CORE CHEMISTRY

Materials

DENISE WALKER

A⁺

Smart Apple Media
an imprint of Black Rabbit Books

This book has been published in cooperation with Evans Publishing Group.

Series editor: Harriet Brown, Editor: Katie Harker, Design: Simon Morse, Illustrations: Ian Thompson, Simon Morse

Published in the United States by Smart Apple Media
2140 Howard Drive West, North Mankato, Minnesota 56003

Library of Congress Cataloging-in-Publication Data

Walker, Denise.
Materials / by Denise Walker.
p. cm. – (Core Chemistry)
Includes index.
ISBN 978-1-58340-817-9
1. Matter—Constitution. 2. Chemical structure. 3. Atoms. I. Title

QC173.W325 2007
530.4—dc22   2006102868

9 8 7 6 5 4 3 2 1

Contents

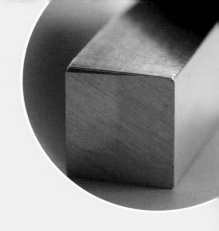

Introduction

The world is made up of many different substances. Thanks to the work of chemists, we are able to make sense of the objects around us. We are surrounded by solids, liquids, and gases that are very different in the way they look and behave. But these physical states all have one thing in common—they are made from tiny particles that are the building blocks of every material on earth.

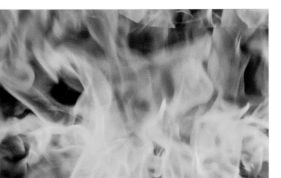

This book explores the wonderful world of materials. You will find out what materials are made of, the way in which particles behave, and how new substances are created. You can also meet famous scientists, such as Ernest Rutherford and Dimitri Mendeleyev; learn how they discovered the existence of particles and found patterns in the behavior of the materials around us.

This book also contains feature boxes that will help you unravel the mysteries of materials. Test yourself on what you have learned so far; investigate some of the concepts discussed; learn key facts; and discover some of the scientific findings of the past and how these might be utilized in the future.

Materials are all around us. Now you can understand why objects look and behave in the ways they do.

DID YOU KNOW?

▶ Look for these boxes. They contain interesting facts about the behavior of materials in the world around us.

TEST YOURSELF

▶ Use these boxes to see how much you've learned. Try to answer the questions without looking at the book, but take a look if you are really stuck.

INVESTIGATE

▶ These boxes contain experiments that you can carry out at home. The equipment you will need is usually inexpensive and easy to find around the house.

TIME TRAVEL

▶ These boxes describe scientific discoveries from the past and fascinating developments that pave the way for the advance of science in the future.

ANSWERS

On pages 46 and 47, you will find the answers to the questions from the "Test yourself" and "Investigate" boxes.

GLOSSARY

Words highlighted in **bold** are described in detail in the glossary on pages 46 and 47.

1

What is matter?

The world around us is composed of a countless number of substances, each in the form of a solid, liquid, or gas. These different substances have distinct properties and ways of behaving. We use some solids as building materials, liquids can be poured into a glass, and some gases help us breathe. Many objects can be broken down into smaller substances; for example, people are composed of bones, blood, and muscles. Chemists study the enormous range of materials in the world and try to explain the changes that take place around us.

▲ Thales believed that water was the basic element from which all things originated. Other philosophers disagreed, claiming that the basic element was air or fire.

WHERE DO MATERIALS COME FROM?

This was a question considered by the ancient Greeks in 600 B.C. Modern scientists can carry out practical experiments to test their ideas, but Greek philosophers preferred to discuss ideas that helped them explain the behavior of the world around them.

The Greeks knew how to extract metals from rocks, and they used fire to change the properties of materials. The Greek philosopher, Thales, suggested that all substances were made from smaller parts, which he called elements. Thales believed that when one substance was turned into another, the elements, as well as the properties of that material, changed.

Other Greek philosophers disagreed with Thales. For example, Anaximander thought that the elements themselves did not change but were in competition with each other. Anaximander suggested that all forms of matter were continually changing because the elements had to compete for dominance.

In 400 B.C., after much debate, Greek philosophers—such as Plato and Aristotle— suggested that there were four types of elements: air, water, earth, and fire. They believed that each of these elements had properties that explained the different materials they produced. For example, "earth" elements, such as metals, had the properties of dryness and coldness and "air" elements, such as gases, had the properties of heat and moistness. This theory became the basis of Western thinking about the natural world for more than 2,000

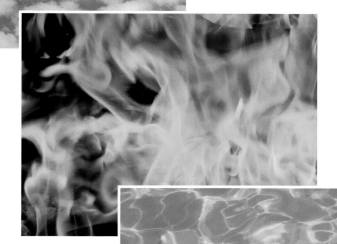

years. In other parts of the world, different elements were suggested. In India, scholars proposed the existence of five elements: space, air, fire, water, and earth. In China, philosophers also conceived of five elements; they were earth, wood, metal, fire, and water. During the rise of chemistry in the 1700s, chemists began to study the composition of rocks and minerals and realized that there were more than just four or five elements. However, even today, the elements proposed by philosophers form the foundation for many Chinese and alternative medical practices.

DISCOVERING PARTICLES

While Plato and Aristotle were discussing the elements, another Greek philosopher, Democritus, suggested the theory that all matter was made up of tiny particles that were so small they could not be seen. Democritus believed that the types of particles, and the way in which they were arranged, determined the final properties of a material. Many people did not believe Democritus because he could not provide evidence for his theory. Today, however, scientific experiments indicate the existence of particles.

If particles are too small to be seen with the naked eye or even with the most powerful microscopes, how do we know they actually exist? The answer

is that we don't, but scientific experiments have strongly indicated that matter is made up of particles. Scientists build theories from scientific evidence, and as time passes, these theories are either proved or disproved. In the case of particle theory, evidence is still being collected, but the theory has yet to be refuted.

Evidence for the existence of particles can be found around us. For example, smoke from a fire or a barbecue does not travel in a straight line. Instead, it slowly floats through the air. Particle theory explains that both smoke and air are composed of tiny particles. As the smoke particles move, they collide with particles in the air and slightly change direction; this movement appears as a random smoke trail.

BROWNIAN MOTION

Scientists can replicate the behavior of smoke in a laboratory. First, a small box, called a smoke cell, is filled with smoke. The smoke cell is viewed under a microscope, where very small particles can be seen moving around. This phenomenon was first observed by the Scottish scientist Robert Brown in 1827 and is called **Brownian motion**. If a bottle of perfume is spilled, and people on the other side of the room are able to smell the fragrance, Brownian motion has occurred. The liquid scent in the perfume has **evaporated** and traveled through the air in a process called diffusion (see page 20). The scent particles travel in exactly the same way as the smoke particles.

▲ The rising smoke from a bonfire indicates that particles of smoke collide with particles of air.

TIME TRAVEL: INTO THE FUTURE

▶ Atomic force microscopy (AFM) is a technique for observing matter that will become widely used in the future. An atomic force microscope doesn't use a lens, like a traditional microscope, but instead uses a probe (or "tip") that closely scans an object's surface to measure properties such as height and magnetism. When the tip encounters a tiny change on the surface, it moves a lever.

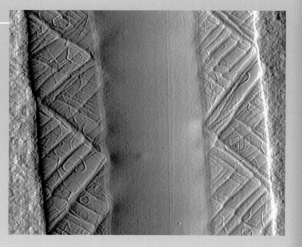

▲ AFM images help scientists observe materials, such as this polymer film, more closely than ever before.

This makes it possible to take measurements of a very small area. A laser beam senses these changes and records them as a map, almost like a photograph. The microscope scans the surface of a sample with such a sensitive touch that it can sometimes even sense the individual atoms on the surface of a crystal, such as gold.

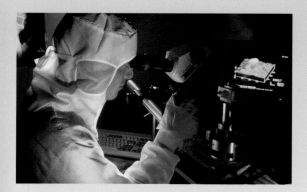

▲ This scientist is using an atomic force microscope to observe the surface of an object in minute detail.

Looking inside the atom

2

During the nineteenth and twentieth centuries, scientists worked to prove that the world is composed of minute particles called **atoms**. They found that there are three types of particles inside an atom. Today, the modern model of the atom is based on what scientists have discovered about the arrangement of these particles.

THE PARTICLES OF AN ATOM

About 100 years ago, scientists first investigated why one substance is different from another. They began by identifying the properties of atoms. Using a beam of **radioactive** particles, called **alpha particles**, they found that almost all of an atom's mass is at its center, which they called the **nucleus**. The scientists discovered the nucleus contains smaller particles called **protons** and **neutrons**. Protons have a positive electric charge, while neutrons have no charge.

Overall, atoms have a neutral charge. Therefore, atoms must contain a negative charge that counteracts the positive charge of the protons; **electrons** carry this negative charge. Electrons circle the nucleus at varying distances. They are attracted to the positively charged nucleus, but because they are constantly moving and relatively light, electrons maintain these distances, creating electron "shells." This arrangement of particles has been likened to planets orbiting the sun in our solar system. Although the planets are attracted by the sun's gravitational pull, they stay in orbit because they are moving so quickly. Scientists now know that substances differ because they have a particular arrangement of protons, neutrons, and electrons.

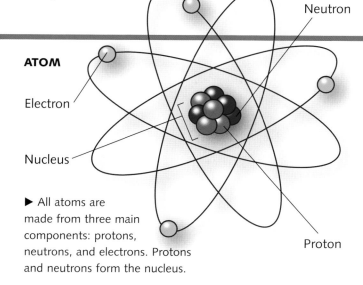

ATOM

Neutron

Electron

Nucleus

Proton

▶ All atoms are made from three main components: protons, neutrons, and electrons. Protons and neutrons form the nucleus.

Summary

Particle	Relative mass	Relative charge
Proton	1	+1
Neutron	1	0
Electron	1/1800	−1

▲ The particles of an atom are extremely light so scientists tend to explain their mass using relative terms.

DID YOU KNOW?

▶ If a sports stadium was an atom, the nucleus would be about the size of a grape in the center circle; consider Yankee Stadium in New York City (below) or Rogers Centre in Toronto, Canada.

TIME TRAVEL: WHAT ARE PARTICLES MADE OF?

All materials on earth are composed of tiny particles that we cannot see with the naked eye. The arrangement of these particles explains why materials are solids, liquids, or gases. What are these tiny particles made of? The work of four scientists, in particular, have helped answer this question.

JOHN DALTON (1766–1844)

John Dalton was an English chemist who used the work of Greek philosophers (such as Democritus) and other scientists (such as Antoine Lavoisier and Joseph Louis Proust) to study the effects of combining two substances to make a new material.

Dalton's work provided scientists with some basic rules about the behavior of particles. His "atomic theory" stated that:

▶ All matter is composed of minute particles called atoms.
▶ Atoms cannot be divided into smaller parts and cannot be destroyed.
▶ Atoms of any element all have the same mass and properties. However, atoms differ from substance to substance.
▶ Atoms combine in simple ratios to form new substances. Dalton called these **compounds**.

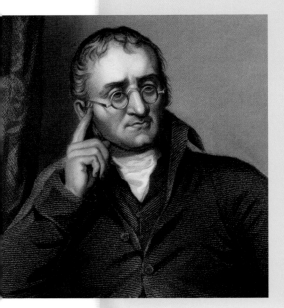

◀ The work of John Dalton was the first published theory suggesting that substances were made from particles. Dalton's ideas were crucial to the development of future work on particle theory.

J. J. THOMSON (1856–1940)

Joseph John Thomson was an English physicist working at Cambridge University in the UK. Thomson explored the composition of particles and atoms. He experimented using currents of electricity—now called cathode rays—traveling through empty glass tubes. Thomson noticed that the currents of electricity changed direction if they were positioned next to a magnet.

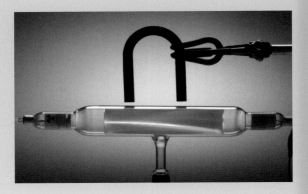

▲ Cathode rays are attracted by a magnetic force. This is because they contain electron particles that are negatively charged.

From these observations, Thomson proposed that the streams of particles were smaller components of atoms, rather than the movement of atoms themselves. This was a bold suggestion at the time because scientists believed that atoms were the basic unit of matter and could not be divided into smaller parts.

Thomson's suggestion was investigated by teams of scientists for many years, and they concluded that cathode rays are streams of electricity composed of electrons—very small, negatively charged particles that are fundamental parts of every atom. The electrons change direction in the presence of magnets because they have a negative charge. Thomson had discovered the negative part of an atom, but he did not know what the inside of an atom looked like. He proposed a "plum pudding" theory, which described the atom as a bed of positive charge (the sponge) in which negative charges (the plums) could be found.

ERNEST RUTHERFORD (1871–1937)

Ernest Rutherford was born in New Zealand but worked for some time at Cambridge University. Rutherford helped to discover the nucleus and identify the positive part of an atom.

In one of his experiments, Rutherford aimed alpha particles—positively charged particles composed of two protons and two neutrons—onto thin pieces of gold leaf. When the alpha particles rebounded from the gold atoms, Rutherford obstructed their path using a zinc sulfide screen. Each time the screen caught an alpha particle, the positive charge caused the zinc to spark. Rutherford made some profound observations:

▶ Most of the alpha particles went straight through the gold leaf, reaching the screen on the other side. Because of this, Rutherford reasoned that most of the gold atoms consisted of space.
▶ Some alpha particles appeared to go through the gold leaf, but were slightly deflected before they hit the screen. Rutherford inferred that part of the atom was positive, and therefore repelled the alpha particles as they passed.
▶ Amazingly, a small number of alpha particles rebounded in the direction from which they came.

THE GOLD LEAF EXPERIMENT

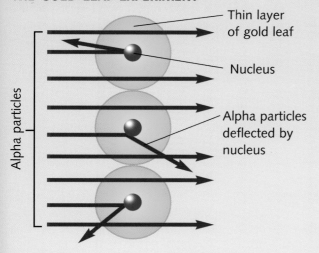

▲ Rutherford's experiment revealed that the gold atoms had a small, dense area in the middle. He called this the nucleus.

From his experiments, Rutherford concluded that the atom did not conform to J. J. Thomson's plum pudding theory, but was mostly space with a small positive charge in the middle. He called the middle of the atom the nucleus and the positive component the proton.

NIELS BOHR (1885–1962)

Niels Bohr was a Danish physicist who worked alongside Rutherford in the early 1900s. Bohr bombarded the atoms of various elements using cathode rays. He observed what happened to the atoms' negatively charged electrons and discovered that different elements produced slightly different patterns. He also noticed that if the energy of the collisions was reduced, the atoms' electrons moved at a slower pace.

From his observations, Bohr was able to deduce that electrons were found in discrete shells surrounding the nucleus of an atom. When the electrons were bombarded with cathode rays, they were able to jump from one shell to the next because they gained energy. When they lost this energy, visible light was emitted. Bohr found that the electrons would not jump to other electron shells if they did not receive the correct amount of energy. This is the important basis of quantum theory—the emission and absorption of energy by matter—that scientists use today.

The work of Dalton, Thomson, Rutherford, and Bohr was an outstanding contribution to our understanding of the material world. However, despite the rapid advancement of their ideas, modern atomic theory was not fully accepted by the scientific community until the early 1900s.

INVESTIGATE

▶ There are many other important scientists who have contributed to the model of the atom that is used today. Research either Albert Einstein or James Chadwick to find out what contributions they have made.

UNDERSTANDING HOW ATOMS DIFFER

We now know that elements differ because they have a unique number of protons, neutrons, and electrons. To help us easily recognize this difference, scientists have assigned two numbers to elements. The larger number is called the **mass number** (or atomic mass). This represents the total number of protons and neutrons in the nucleus of an element's atom. The smaller number is called the **atomic number**. This represents only the number of protons contained in the atom. Since atoms have a neutral charge, we assume that the number of protons is equal to the number of electrons (because they have equal, but opposite charges).

For example, the metal lithium has been assigned an atomic number of 3 and a mass number of 7. This means that lithium atoms have three protons (atomic number), three electrons (equivalent to atomic number), and four neutrons (mass number minus atomic number). Similarly, the metal beryllium has been assigned an atomic

▲◄ Lithium (above) and beryllium (left) are both metals but their varying atomic structure means that they have very different properties.

number of four and a mass number of nine. This means that beryllium atoms have four protons, four electrons, and five neutrons. Because lithium and beryllium atoms have a different number of protons, neutrons, and electrons, the metals have very different properties.

DID YOU KNOW?

▶ Scientists in Switzerland have shown that it is possible for two identical particles to respond simultaneously to a stimulus that one particle receives, even if they are over 6.2 miles (10 km) apart. The scientists at the University of Geneva split particles of light, called photons, into pairs and sent them down separate optical fibers (telephone lines). Despite being separated by a number of miles, each particle chose the same path down their respective optical fiber. The experiment confirms a theory that Austrian physicist Erwin Schrödinger predicted: Entangled particles—particles that are formed at the same time and have identical properties—echo each other's actions, no matter how far apart they are. Scientists think that a change in one particle will affect the other, even if it is on the opposite side of the universe.

INVESTIGATE

▶ Research the atomic number and the mass number of each of the following elements. How many protons, neutrons, and electrons do the atoms of each element have?

(1) Magnesium
(2) Bromine
(3) Neon

The modern model of the atom was proposed by Niels Bohr in 1913, yet scientists have wondered whether there are more than three types of atomic particles. As experimental technology has developed, this search has brought many new discoveries.

In 1995, the Nobel prize for physics was awarded to two California research centers for the discovery of two of the smallest particles in the universe. During the 1950s, Frederick Reines and his colleagues at the University of California were able to demonstrate the existence of a particle called the **neutrino** (the "little neutral one"). This particle has no mass or electrical charge, so it is very difficult to detect. Scientists suspected the neutrino's existence because they noticed the presence of mystery particles produced when radioactive materials decayed. Reines and his colleague, Clyde Cowan, attempted to prove the existence of the neutrino.

Working at the Savannah River nuclear reactor 39 feet (12 m) underground, Reines and Cowan discovered the neutrino in 1956. They waited for what they believed would be a neutrino particle from a nuclear reaction to hit a tank of water. The water contained cadmium chloride; cadmium chloride is highly soluble in water and easily absorbs particles. When the cadmium chloride absorbs the neutrino particles, it emits high-frequency electromagnetic radiation, which can be detected. Reines and Cowan confirmed the existence of the neutrino particles by observing these changes following a nuclear reaction. Today, scientists believe that neutrinos affect the motion of galaxies and play a key role in the nuclear fusion that causes stars to burn (see page 29).

In 1977, another subatomic particle was discovered by Martin Perl and his colleagues at Stanford University. For three years, Perl and his team conducted a series of experiments, which recorded the effects of colliding different particles. During these experiments, the team discovered an unknown particle that was electrically charged, about 3,500 times heavier than an electron, and that had a very short life span. The particle was later named "tau."

Today, similar collision experiments are carried out in Switzerland at the European Center for Nuclear Research (CERN). Here, particles of all descriptions are bombarded and collided for research groups who are searching for new particles. The center has a large circular tunnel, located within the mountains. The circumference of the tunnel is 17 miles (27 km). Around the edges of the tunnel, 5,000 magnets are used to make the circulating particles move faster. To date, 12 subatomic particles have been discovered; the latest of these is called the "top quark." The top quark is a heavy particle that existed for a brief time following the creation of the universe. In 1992, a team of international scientists simulated this explosion by colliding trillions of subatomic particles. This simulation proved the existence of the top quark.

▼ **Specialized equipment has been installed in underground tunnels at CERN to investigate atomic particles.**

In the early 1900s, Niels Bohr announced a theory to explain how electrons are arranged in the atom. He suggested that electrons were positioned in shells at varying distances around the nucleus and that these shells of electrons had a particular level of energy. Electron shells are sometimes called energy levels. Bohr thought it was possible to move an electron from one shell to another by applying an exact amount of energy. His ideas formed the basis of many modern theories about the behavior of electrons in atoms.

Because of Bohr's theory, scientists have discovered some interesting patterns in electron behavior. For example, electron shells in an atom have the following properties:

▶ Each shell contains electrons that have the same energy level.

▶ Electron shells closest to the nucleus have the lowest energy level.

▶ Shells with the lowest energy level fill with electrons first.

▶ Electron shells farther from the nucleus have smaller energy gaps between them than those closer to the nucleus.

▶ Each electron shell holds a maximum number of electrons. Some of these are shown below.

Electron shell	Maximum number of electrons
First (closest to nucleus)	2
Second	8
Third	18

▶ The electrons closest to the nucleus are difficult to move because they are strongly attracted to the positive charge of the nucleus.

ELECTRON SHELLS

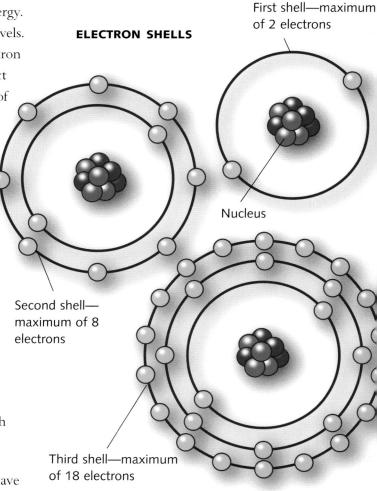

First shell—maximum of 2 electrons

Nucleus

Second shell— maximum of 8 electrons

Third shell—maximum of 18 electrons

▲ Electrons are arranged around the nucleus at varying distances. We call these electron shells. The electrons have increasing levels of energy as they move away from the nucleus.

ELECTRON CONFIGURATION

Different atoms have different numbers of occupied electron shells. For example, hydrogen atoms have one occupied electron shell, while uranium atoms have seven. The way electrons are arranged in the atom is called the **electron configuration**. The atomic number tells us the number of protons, which is equal to the number of electrons in a neutrally charged atom.

This information is used to calculate the electron configuration of the atom. For example, carbon's atomic number is "6," so carbon has six protons and six electrons. Electrons always fill the shells closest to the nucleus first. However, because the first electron shell holds a maximum of two electrons, the remaining four carbon electrons move to the second shell. (This shell is not completely full because a maximum of eight electrons can be held at this level.)

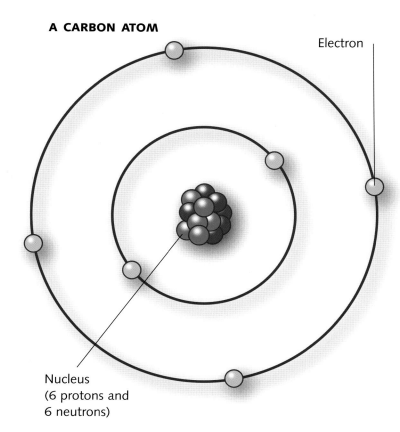

Electron

Nucleus
(6 protons and
6 neutrons)

THE IMPORTANCE OF ELECTRON CONFIGURATION

The materials around us are formed when elements combine to form **molecules** and compounds. The atoms in molecules and compounds bond when electrons move within and between atoms during a chemical reaction. Electrons and protons have opposite charges and they are balanced if they are equal in number. However, if these charges become imbalanced, the electrons rearrange themselves between atoms so that they become more stable. Some atoms share electrons and become a new substance, while others release electrons or remove them from other atoms. In some cases, this rearrangement links the atoms to form molecules. We call this **bonding**. During chemical bonding, atoms try to acquire the maximum number of electrons in their outer shells.

Chemical reactions are different from nuclear reactions. Chemical reactions are caused by a change in electron configuration, while nuclear reactions are caused by a change in the nucleus of an atom, with protons and neutrons either lost or gained. Chemists are interested in chemical reactions and try to explain these reactions using the theory of electron configuration.

3

Solids, liquids, and gases

Many materials in the world around us are solids. All solids have a number of similar properties: They tend to hold their shape unless a force is applied, and they are relatively strong. The clothes we wear and the chairs we sit on are examples of solids. These materials have a particular shape. Other solids are used as building materials because they are strong enough to withstand storms and high winds. All solids possess a certain degree of strength; it is mainly this quality that distinguishes solids from liquids and gases.

A CLOSER LOOK AT SOLIDS

If we could observe solids from the point of view of an atom, we would see that the particles are closely packed together.

According to particle theory, the particles in solids are arranged in tightly fixed and regular positions. The particles are held in these positions by strong forces. We call these **intermolecular** forces of attraction. These forces occur when the protons of one atom attract the electrons of another atom. Although the particles are not able to leave their positions, they can vibrate around a fixed point.

This arrangement of particles produces solids with the following properties:

▶ Solids are usually strong. When pressure is applied to a solid, the strong forces of attraction between the atoms are not easily broken.

▶ Solids hold their shape because the particles are so firmly held together that they can only vibrate.

▶ Solids cannot be poured because the particles are compressed and do not separate from each other.

▶ Because the particles of a solid are not free to move like those of a gas or liquid, solids cannot exert any pressure against the sides of a container.

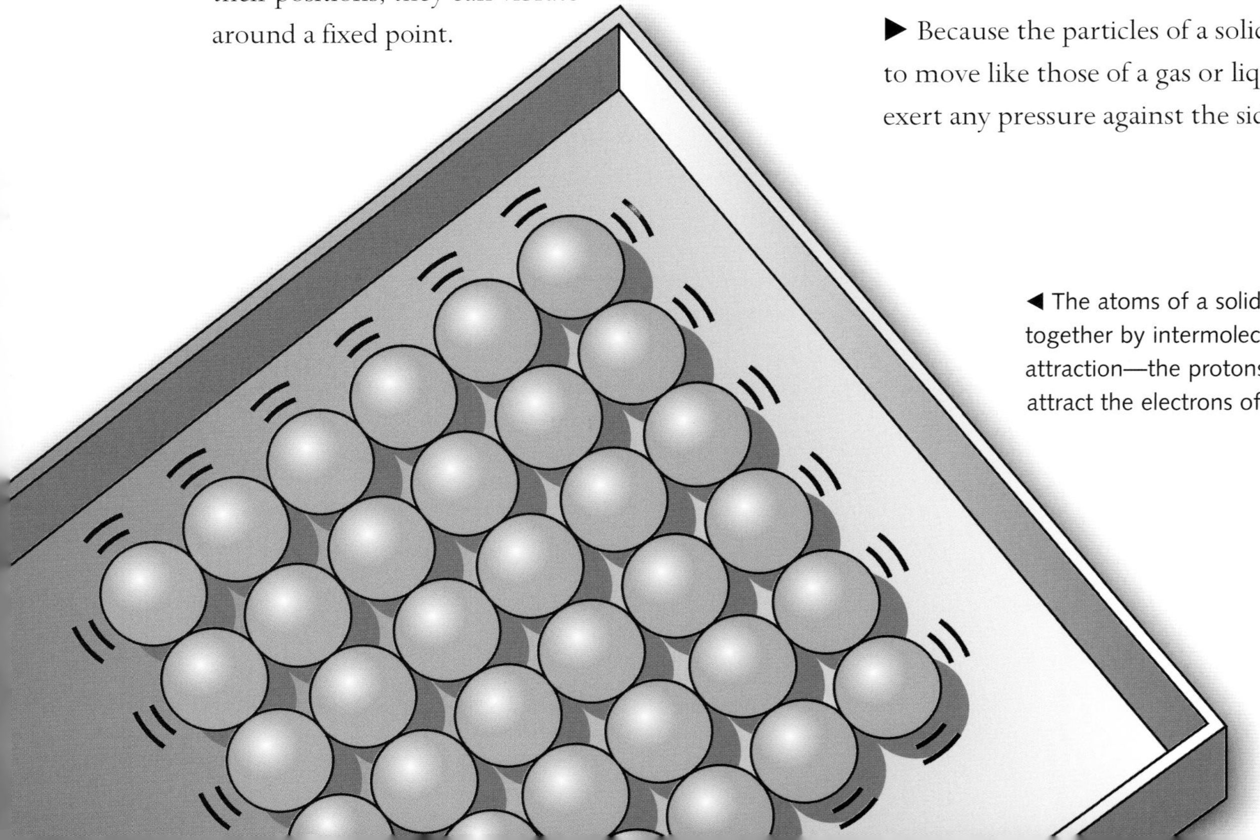

◀ The atoms of a solid are closely held together by intermolecular forces of attraction—the protons of one atom attract the electrons of another atom.

All solids demonstrate these properties. However, some solids are more difficult to recognize. Can you think of any examples?

Sand is one example of a solid that is similar to a liquid because it can be poured. If you examine sand carefully you will see that it is made of very small, solid grains. Individual grains of sand cannot be poured, but a collection of sand grains can be poured.

Custard is a liquid, but it also demonstrates some properties of a solid. If custard is made from flour, which has a starch base, it can be made so thick that it is strong enough to walk on. However, a custard mixture of this kind cannot support a large amount of pressure. If you stopped walking on the custard, the force of your weight concentrated in one area would cause you to sink.

TEST YOURSELF

▶ In what ways can each of the following substances be described as a solid? In what ways are they not typical solids?

(1) Jelly
(2) Paste
(3) Glue stick

◀ ▲ Custard is a liquid, but it can be made so that it is strong enough to walk on. However, if you stop walking, you quickly sink in!

DID YOU KNOW?

▶ Have you seen movies with characters sinking in quicksand? It looks frightening, but scientifically, quicksand isn't as dangerous as it seems. Quicksand occurs wherever there is sand or soil and water. The sand stays solid when the individual grains are in contact with each other. But when sand becomes saturated with water, the grains no longer touch and they begin to move around and act like a liquid. Quicksand looks solid, but when someone steps on it they sink. This is because the water is pushed up through the sand and the grains become separated. If the person then starts to struggle, this process is accelerated and they sink even farther. However, sand is more dense than water, so it is easier to float in saturated sand than in water.

▲ Quicksand looks solid enough to walk on, but it can be dangerous if you start to sink!

A CLOSER LOOK AT LIQUIDS

Like solids, liquids are all around us. About 70 percent of the earth's surface is covered by ocean water and almost two-thirds of the human body contains water. But liquids have distinctly different properties from solids. For example, liquids allow solids to pass through them. Marine animals swim through ocean water to survive and blood circulates around the body to keep us alive. Liquids also flow from one place to another under the influence of gravity.

If we could observe liquids from an atomic point of view, we would see that liquid particles are more spread out than solid particles. Particle theory asserts that liquid particles are held together in small groups because most of the strong intermolecular forces of attraction present in solids have been broken down. Liquid particles contain more energy than solid particles, giving them a greater ability to move. The small groups of liquid particles can slide past each other, but because there are still some forces of attraction present, the

particles are not completely free to move around. This arrangement of particles produces liquids with the following properties:

▶ Liquids cannot hold objects because they are not strong enough. If we touch a liquid, our hand will pass through. This is because there are few forces of attraction between the particles.

▶ Liquids cannot hold their shape because the particles are free to move. Liquids will fill and conform to the shape of their containers.

▶ Liquids can be poured because the particles are free to move.

▶ Liquids can be compressed slightly because pressure pushes the particles closer together. For example, if you take a syringe that is half filled with water and block the end, when you try to push the plunger down, the water will be slightly compressed because it is pushed into a smaller space.

▶ Small quantities of liquids do not exert much pressure. This is because the particles are not completely free to move and collide with the wall of a container. However, if the container is filled completely, the liquid exerts more pressure. The water pressure increases with the amount of water in a container. For example, there is an enormous amount of water pressure at the bottom of the ocean. There is not much marine life at this depth because their bodies would be crushed by the force of the water.

▼ The atoms in a liquid are free to move around but are held together in groups by intermolecular forces.

UNUSUAL LIQUIDS

Some liquids are described as **volatile**. This means they easily turn into gases. For example, we smell gasoline fumes at a gas station because gasoline is a volatile liquid and some of its particles evaporate rapidly into the air. Other liquids are nonvolatile. For example, molasses is a thick, syrup-like substance that can be poured slowly but will not evaporate.

The difference between gasoline and molasses is attributed to the level of "stickiness" in their particles. In gasoline, the particles are arranged in smaller groups than in molasses. With fewer intermolecular forces of attraction, the gasoline particles are more likely to evaporate. In contrast, the groups of particles in molasses are more compact, making this liquid difficult to pour.

Glass objects, such as ornaments and windows, are made from liquid glass that cools to become a solid. To make an ornament, a glass blower molds the liquid mixture before it is allowed to cool. Scientists have found that some glass windows melt on very hot days; a windowpane of glass can become thinner at the top and thicker at the bottom.

Mercury is an unusual metal because it is liquid at room temperature. Metals are usually strong, hard materials. Mercury is so heavy and dense that objects such as bricks and pieces of lead can float in it! Mercury freezes at about -36.4°F (-38°C) and boils at about 674.6°F (357°C).

A CLOSER LOOK AT GASES

The air that fills our lungs is probably the gas that we are most familiar with. Air displays many of the properties explained by particle theory. The air cannot be seen, smelled, or tasted and we often take its presence for granted. However, gases such as air play a very important role in our survival.

Gases have a much more random arrangement of particles than liquids and solids. Particle theory maintains that there are no forces of attraction between gas particles and that gas particles contain much more energy than liquid or solid particles. Gas particles are constantly moving, and if we could see them, they would have a random appearance—no two gases at any one moment have exactly the same arrangement of particles.

This arrangement of particles produces gases with the following properties:

▶ There are no forces of attraction between gas particles. We cannot press or sit on a gas because there are no forces holding the particles together. When we touch a gas, the particles move away from our fingers.

▶ Gases do not hold their shape. Gas particles will move to fill a container that they are stored in. Every gas particle has its own path and enough energy to keep it moving. When gas particles meet the wall of a container, or each other, they simply bounce off and pursue a new path.

▶ Most gases cannot be poured. The particles in gases are free to move around and are, therefore, difficult to contain. It is only possible to pour a gas of greater density into a gas that is less dense.

▶ Gases exert pressure. Gas particles constantly move around and collide with the walls of their container. As they do so, they create pressure. The more gas particles that are present in a container, the more the pressure increases. The tires of a car, for example, are filled with air; when the tires are inflated, the tire pressure increases.

▶ Gases diffuse. This means that they travel from an area where there is a lot of gas, to an area where there is very little. Perfume scent travels through the air by a process of diffusion. Diffusion occurs in the animal world, too. Many animals can detect each other from far away by the chemicals they secrete.

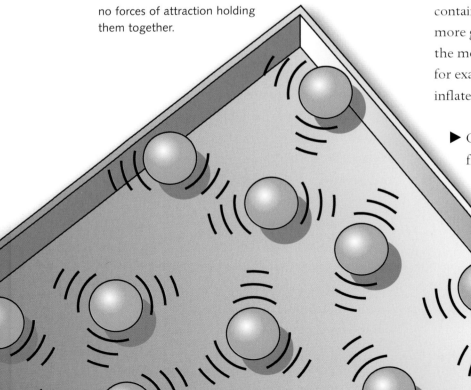

▼ The atoms in a gas are free to move around because there are no forces of attraction holding them together.

These chemical secretions evaporate into gases, and although they are diluted, they can be detected from very long distances. For example, some moths can detect scents from up to three miles (5 km) away to help them find a mate. Dogs and cats use scent to identify their territory for other animals.

▶ Gases can be compressed. Although they are constantly moving at high speeds, gas particles keep a lot of space between them. This is because the forces of attraction that hold the particles together are overcome by the energy of the moving particles. If a gas is trapped within a container and pressurized, the particles move together and become compressed. If the particles move close enough together, the compressed gas becomes a liquid. Some gases, such as butane, are compressed and stored as liquids because the liquid takes up less space and is easier to transport.

◀ Propane is compressed into a liquid so that it can be easily stored and transported.

▼ This satellite image shows the expanse of the smoke cloud after the Buncefield Oil Depot explosion. The smoke drifted 9,843 feet (3,000 m) high, covering much of southern England.

▲ The Buncefield Oil Depot fire in 2005 produced smoke covering an area of more than 74 miles (119 km).

DID YOU KNOW?

▶ In 2005, an explosion at the Buncefield Oil Depot in the UK was caused by an overfilled fuel tank that allowed fuel to escape and clouds of vapor to form. Fuels are volatile liquids that evaporate into gases at room temperature. Fuel as a gas is highly flammable and a small spark can start a fire. Once the fumes ignite, the liquid fuel also catches fire. Smoking is not permitted at gas stations for this reason.

▶ In the 1800s, Italian chemist Amedeo Avogadro discovered that any gas (at the same temperature and pressure) contains the same number of particles. Gases are very light, but a cubic foot of gas, such as air, contains billions of particles. In order to describe these large numbers, chemists use a measurement called the mole, or "Avogadro's number." During his studies, Avogadro found that 1 gram of hydrogen had the same number of particles as 12 grams of carbon. This was approximately 6.022×10^{23} particles, or one "mole" of particles. One cubic foot (0.03 cu m) of air contains about 1.1 moles of particles.

4

The symbols of chemistry

In the middle ages, chemists were called alchemists. When the alchemists carried out their experiments, they assigned a symbol to the substances they used and produced so that they could easily communicate their results to others. Originally, the alchemists employed the symbols for the planets because, at the time, there was a close link between astronomy and the study of the material world.

▲ Alchemists often worked in secret because they were regarded with suspicion. Their work, however, helped lay the foundation of modern chemistry.

Alchemists used distinct symbols for the metals they worked with. For example, gold was considered to be the most pure substance because it did not react with anything. Therefore, the symbol for gold was a complete circle—round like the sun, with a golden-yellow color. Silver, thought to be almost pure, was

given the symbol of a crescent moon—not quite a perfect circle. Also, silver reflects a silvery light, much like the moon. Medieval alchemists were considered magicians because they could create unknown substances. Many alchemists were subject to persecution, so they invented secret symbols to record their work. Over time, the science of **alchemy** became dominated by fraudulent practices.

MODERN SYMBOLS

In 1787, Antoine Lavoisier wrote a book naming all the chemical symbols known at the time. In 1813, Swedish chemist Jöns Berzelius began to assign each of these substances a symbol, based on the

Metal	Planet symbol	Illustrated symbol
Gold	Sun	☉
Silver	Moon	☽
Mercury	Mercury	☿
Tin	Jupiter	♃
Lead	Saturn	♄
Copper	Venus	♀
Iron	Mars	♂

first letter of its name. If elements began with the same letter, Berzelius added the second letter of the elements. For example, bismuth was given the symbol Bi and beryllium the symbol Be. Notice that when there are two letters in a chemical symbol, the first letter is always in upper case and the second letter is in lower case.

Sometimes, chemical names originate from Latin, so the chemical symbols are taken from the Latin, rather than the English, word.
For example:

Element	Latin name	Symbol
Iron	Ferrum	Fe
Silver	Argentum	Ag
Gold	Aurum	Au
Copper	Cuprum	Cu

Other elements are named and assigned symbols based on their chemical or physical properties. For example, the term chlorine (Cl) comes from the Greek word *chlôros* (green). Bromine (Br) comes from the Greek word *brômos* (stench), because it has a strong smell.

Some elements are named after places or people. For example, strontium (Sr) is named after a village in Scotland (Strontian) where this element was first identified in rock material taken from a mine. Uranium (U) was named in honor of the discovery of the planet Uranus. Einsteinium (Es) is named after the famous scientist, Albert Einstein. We also have californium (Cf), discovered by a research group working at the University of California, Berkeley.

CHOOSING NAMES FOR NEW ELEMENTS

An international committee called IUPAC (the International Union of Pure and Applied Chemistry) oversees the naming of new elements and compounds. When a new element is found, researchers formally propose a name for their discovery. These names are usually based on a myth or classical character, a mineral, a place, a property of the element, or a famous scientist. A proposed name is discussed by IUPAC before becoming internationally accepted as the official name. It is important that chemical symbols are universally understood so that chemists around the world can easily communicate with each other.

In 1974, a dispute about the naming of element 104 was mediated by IUPAC. Element 104 was discovered by two separate research groups. The Russian group wanted to call the element Dubnium (Db), while the American group wanted to call it Rutherfordium (Rf), in honor of the scientist, Ernest Rutherford. IUPAC declared that element 104 should be named Unnilquadium, from the Latin terms *un* (1), *nil* (0), and *quad* (4). This name was kept until 1997, when the matter was finally resolved and the element became Rutherfordium (Rf).

INVESTIGATE

▶ Research the names for these chemical symbols.

▶ Now find the chemical symbol for these elements.

(1) Na

(2) Mg

(3) Zn

(4) I

(5) Scandium

(6) Sulfur

(7) Antimony

(8) Lead

THE PERIODIC TABLE

Elements are basic matter that cannot be broken down into simpler substances, but they combine to make the materials we see around us. For example, the metal aluminum is an element made from only aluminum atoms. Oxygen is a gas made from only oxygen atoms. The different arrangement of particles in aluminum and oxygen atoms explains why these two elements have such contrasting properties.

One of the most important tools in chemistry is the **periodic table**. This table does more than list all the known elements; it has been designed to group together similar types of elements and it provides flexibility to add more elements as they are discovered.

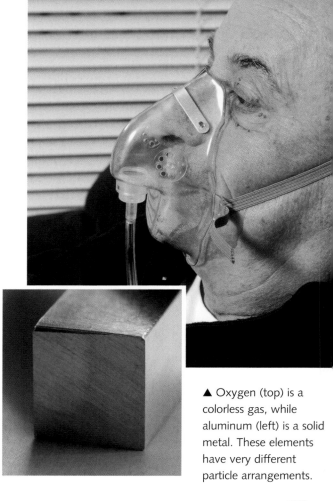

▲ Oxygen (top) is a colorless gas, while aluminum (left) is a solid metal. These elements have very different particle arrangements.

THE PERIODIC TABLE

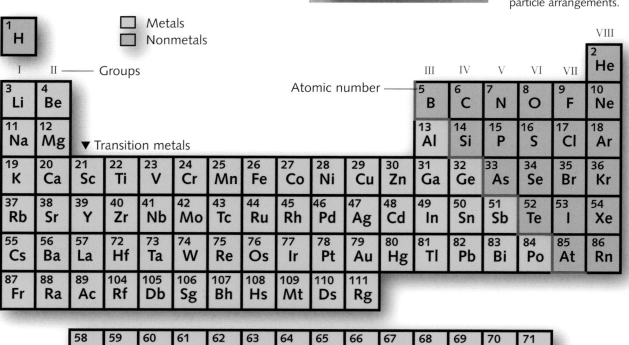

24

The periodic table contains some of the following features:

▶ Elements are organized into vertical columns (**groups**) and horizontal rows (**periods**). There are eight main groups. They are organized around the central block, called the "transition metals." There are seven periods.

▶ Common elements are broadly classified as metals and nonmetals. As a rough guide, elements on the right side of the table are nonmetals, and those on the left are metals. Now, look at some elements that are unfamiliar, such as selenium (Se). This is found on the right of the table, so it is likely to be a nonmetal.

▶ The elements in the table are organized so that the vertical groups contain elements with similar properties. Understanding the properties of one element in a group, enables scientists to predict the properties—and behavior—of the other elements in that group.

▶ The table is called "periodic" because it arranges the elements in such a way that properties are repeated at fixed intervals. For example, if lithium (Li) has a particular property, there are another eight elements on the table before the same property appears in another element—in this case sodium (Na), which sits below lithium. Eight elements after sodium is potassium (K), with the same property as lithium and sodium. After potassium, the interval increases to 18 elements, but the periodic properties remain the same.

▶ Elements in the seventh row of the table contain atoms with many protons and neutrons in their nucleus. These elements are radioactive. Their nuclei spontaneously disintegrate, emitting high-energy particles. These elements are unstable because they do not have enough neutrons to balance the protons in the nucleus. If an atom is bombarded with radioactive particles, some of the protons may be removed from the nucleus, altering the composition of the atom. Changing the atomic structure of a nucleus results in a completely different element.

INVESTIGATE

▶ Choose an element that is unknown to you from the periodic table, but is in the same group as one you are more familiar with. Is it a nonmetal or a metal? Make some predictions about the behavior of the unfamiliar element. Check your predictions using the Internet. Is the periodic table a useful tool?

DID YOU KNOW?

▶ Six elements compose nearly all (99 percent) of the human body: calcium, hydrogen, carbon, phosphorous, oxygen, and nitrogen. The body also contains many other elements in small amounts, such as potassium, sulfur, sodium, and magnesium. We replenish our body with these important substances by eating a balanced diet. Two-thirds of the body is composed of water, so hydrogen and oxygen are the most common elements.

▶ In 1980, Dr. Glenn Seaborg changed a few thousand atoms of lead into gold using a nuclear reactor. Seaborg used high-energy particles to split the nuclei of lead atoms so that they released three protons. Gold has three fewer protons than lead (79, compared to 82). However, Seaborg's experiment required an enormous amount of energy so this form of gold would be far too expensive to produce commercially.

TIME TRAVEL: DEVELOPING THE PERIODIC TABLE

The modern periodic table is the result of work by a number of prominent scientists. The periodic table has a unique structure and order that was derived from observations of the few elements that were known to scientists when the table was first designed. The actual shape of the current table is similar to the first table. The final design was approved by an international committee in 1985, after years of discussion. The format of the periodic table allows new elements to be added. Chemists also use "ingredients" from the periodic table to build molecules that have never before existed on the earth.

Since the discovery of the first element, scientists have been classifying elements according to their properties. At first, this was simply a case of comparing metals with gases, but as more elements were discovered, this basic classification became more difficult.

ATTEMPTING TO CLASSIFY THE ELEMENTS

▶ In 1829, a German scientist named Johann Döbereiner announced his "Law of Triads" in an attempt to classify the elements more precisely. This law classified elements in three groups that had similar chemical properties. Using the Law of Triads, the properties of the middle element could be predicted based on the properties of the elements on either side of it.

▶ In 1843, the ideas of Döbereiner were expanded upon when German chemist Leopold Gmelin published his work. Gmelin also grouped elements, but he formed three groups of four elements and one group of five—the latter included nitrogen and phosphorus and later became the fifth group of the modern periodic table.

▶ Groups of three, four, or five elements were the only progress made at this time because scientists had yet to discover atomic mass—a property common to all elements. Atomic mass was discovered by Italian chemist Stanislao Cannizzaro in 1858. Although scientists could not weigh individual atoms, they had found a way to use electricity to split molecules into individual atoms, so they could be compared. Cannizzaro gave hydrogen—the first element on the periodic table—a value of "one," and assigned an atomic mass to the other elements based on this first value.

▶ In 1865, English scientist John Newlands made more progress toward the modern periodic table by suggesting the "Law of Octaves." Newlands recognized the pattern of chemical properties repeated every eight elements but was not able to order the elements in their current irregular structure. Also Newlands's table did not account for the discovery of additional elements, which was a major flaw in his theory.

▼ Part of Newlands's table (below). The table showed repeating patterns, but the metal iron (Fe) was in the same group as two nonmetals, oxygen (O) and sulfur (S).

H	Li	Be	B	C	N	O
F	Na	Mg	Al	Si	P	S
Cl	K	Ca	Cr	Ti	Mn	Fe

DIMITRI MENDELEYEV

In February 1869, the Russian chemist Dimitri Mendeleyev wrote each element and its chief properties on separate cards and began to lay the cards out in various patterns. Mendeleyev put the lightest element (hydrogen) in the top left corner and the heaviest atom in the bottom right corner. He formed a new line every time he came to an element that had properties similar to hydrogen. The pattern that he finally settled upon had similar elements grouped in vertical columns, unlike his first table, which grouped them horizontally.

The layout of Mendeleyev's table produced some interesting developments in the evolution of the periodic table:

▶ Space was provided for new elements. Mendeleyev was confident in his arrangement of elements so he left space on the table for undiscovered elements. He also used elements around the spaces to predict the properties of the undiscovered elements. Using his table, he predicted the properties of three unknown elements, and within six years, scandium, gallium, and germanium were discovered. His most famous prediction was gallium. Mendeleyev predicted that gallium had a density of 5.9 grams per cubic centimeter. Gallium was discovered in 1875. Later, its **density** was measured at 5.956 grams per cubic centimeter—matching Mendeleyev's prediction.

▶ Some elements were placed in the incorrect groups. Before Mendeleyev's work, beryllium oxide (an oxide of the element beryllium) was expressed using the chemical formula Be_2O_3. This would have placed beryllium in group III of Mendeleyev's table. However, with no space in group III, Mendeleyev placed beryllium in group II because it shared this group's properties. Years later, scientists discovered that beryllium oxide has the formula BeO. Mendeleyev had correctly placed beryllium in group II.

▶ Some elements were listed on the periodic table in the wrong order, according to their atomic mass. Mendeleyev placed elements according to their properties. For example, he put tellurium (Te) before

▲ Although other chemists had recognized patterns in the properties of elements, Dimitri Mendeleyev was the first to realize the significance of these patterns.

iodine (I) even though tellurium is heavier than iodine. Mendeleyev grouped the elements this way because their respective chemical properties corresponded with the other elements in their groups. Mendeleyev presumed that the mass of tellurium had been incorrectly calculated. The mass was correct, but many years later, scientists discovered another atom of tellurium that had a different atomic mass—and it was heavier than iodine! This phenomenon has occurred with three other pairs of elements in the periodic table, when new elements were discovered.

INVESTIGATE

▶ When Mendeleyev created his table, only 65 elements were known. Today, the periodic table contains 111 elements. In addition to tellurium and iodine, there are three other pairs of elements that are out of order according to atomic mass. Can you find these pairs of elements on the Internet?

5

Discovering the elements

When Mendeleyev created his periodic table in 1869, 65 elements were known. Another 14 elements were discovered in Mendeleyev's lifetime, giving him the satisfaction of knowing that his predictions were largely correct. Following his death in 1907, eight more elements were discovered and 24 were created artificially under laboratory conditions. The majority of these new elements are very heavy and are located at the bottom of the periodic table.

▶ Lead

ALCHEMY

Alchemy is considered to be the precursor of chemistry. An art that was handed down through the centuries, alchemy originated in ancient Egypt. *Al-chemia* is an Arabic word that means "to pour or cast together." Alchemy quickly spread through Spain and the rest of Europe and was also developed in China. The alchemists were fascinated by the elements. In particular, they spent much of their time in search of the "philosopher's stone." The alchemists thought this unknown substance had the power to turn lead into gold and held the secret of eternal youth and good health.

◀ Tin

▼ Mercury

OTHER ANCIENT ELEMENTS

The alchemists experimented with substances by heating and mixing them together. They discovered some of the elements, such as iron, mercury, tin, lead, silver, gold, and copper. However, other elements present at the time remained undiscovered because they were inaccessible. For example, the alchemists did not discover hydrogen, because in its pure form it is a colorless, odorless gas that is not easy to detect. Hydrogen is mainly found combined with oxygen in the form of water. Hydrogen was eventually discovered in 1766 by the English chemist Henry Cavendish. When Cavendish experimented with acids and mercury he found that these substances reacted to produce hydrogen gas.

▼ Gold

▼ Copper

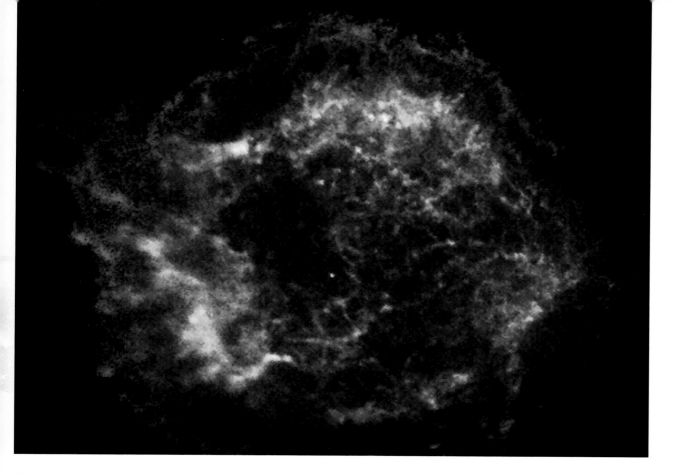

HIDDEN ELEMENTS

Some elements result from the behavior of other elements. For example, when hydrogen atoms collide at high speed, they stick together and form heavier atoms of the element helium. This process is called **fusion** and forms the basis of every star in the night sky. Stars are made of hydrogen gas that is pulled together by the force of gravity. In the smallest stars, hydrogen fuses to form helium. In medium-sized stars, helium fuses to form oxygen and carbon, and in larger stars, heavier elements such as neon, sodium, sulfur, and iron are formed.

Elements heavier than iron cannot become a star through fusion. Instead, these heavier atoms are created in a huge explosion—a supernova—at the end of the life of a very large star, called a "blue giant." Astronomers have studied supernovae and stars to see the elements that

▲ During a supernova, elements heavier than iron are made and scattered into the universe.

they contain using a technique called spectroscopy. Spectroscopy detects the emission of light rays and other electromagnetic particles. Many elements have been discovered in space using spectroscopy, including some very reactive elements, such as cesium and rubidium.

THE SEARCH FOR NONREACTIVE ELEMENTS

Nonreactive elements have been more difficult to find. For example, argon—a colorless, odorless, nonreactive gas—was discovered in 1894 when English chemists William Ramsay and Lord Rayleigh experimented with liquefied air. They discovered that a mystery element (argon) accounted for about one percent of air. Their finding soon led to the discovery of other inert gases, found on the right side of the periodic table.

FINDING HIGHLY REACTIVE ELEMENTS

Many of our most reactive metals combine tightly with other elements in the earth's crust, so they are difficult to find and extract. For example, aluminum metal was not found until 1825. Aluminum can only be extracted from its ore by the use of electricity, which was not fully developed until the 1800s.

FINDING ELEMENTS USING RADIOACTIVITY

Radioactivity is a process caused by the nuclei of certain atoms breaking down and emitting smaller particles. This process has occurred for billions of years. However, some radioactive elements, such as radium and polonium, were discovered as recently as 1898, when Pierre and Marie Curie identified them. At the time, radioactivity in uranium ore had been a recent discovery. However, while extracting uranium from its ore, the Curies noticed that the waste material was also radioactive, suggesting the presence of other elements.

◀ Pierre and Marie Curie extracted the radioactive elements radium and polonium from uranium ore.

MAKING ELEMENTS

The last 24 elements of the periodic table have been created in the laboratory, rather than discovered as natural elements on the earth.

INVESTIGATE

▶ Examine the periodic table and choose an element you do not know. Research how this element was discovered. Was it discovered using electricity, radioactivity, spectroscopy, or some other means?

Although synthetic, these are still considered to be elements because they are composed of only one type of atom. One of the difficulties in creating new elements is that the nuclei are so heavy they are unstable—and therefore short-lived. These elements are usually made by bombarding other elements with atoms or parts of atoms. An example of a synthetic element is curium. This element was produced in 1994 by scientists in the United States. It is named after the Curies and is now used in satellite technology.

DID YOU KNOW?

▶ The sun is a star, but it is too small to form a supernova; only stars that are at least eight times larger than our sun end as supernovae. Fortunately, the sun will not explode. However, stars lose some of their matter as energy during the process of fusion—the sun has already utilized about half of its hydrogen, and in another five billion years, the sun's hydrogen will be depleted. When this occurs, the sun will expand to form what astronomers call a "red giant," absorbing planets, such as Mercury, Venus, and eventually, Earth. The sun will then cool, shrink, and disappear.

▶ American scientist, Dr. Glenn Seaborg (1912–99), contributed to the discovery of 10 elements in the periodic table—a contribution to chemistry beyond that of any other person. Seaborg discovered plutonium and codiscovered another element, seaborgium, which is named after him. Seaborg also discovered almost 100 different forms of known elements, called isotopes.

Changing physical states

6

Gases, liquids, and solids have very different properties because their particles are arranged in different ways. To change from one physical state to another, heat energy is usually required. If you take an ice cube from the freezer, for example, it will eventually turn into a small pool of water at room temperature. The heat from the room has caused the solid water (ice) to turn into liquid water. Heating the pool of water further would cause it to boil and evaporate into a gas (steam). Pressure can also be used to change a substance from one physical state into another.

CHANGING BETWEEN LIQUIDS AND GASES

LIQUID TO GAS

When it rains, puddles form that are mostly liquid water. The sun dries these puddles gradually. As the sun shines, the warmth heats the particles in the puddle so that they gain more energy. This increase in energy causes the particles to vibrate and break free from the intermolecular forces of attraction that bind them. Eventually, the particles break away from each other. When particles overcome the forces of attraction, they escape from the liquid—this is called evaporation. Evaporation occurs only at the surface of a liquid.

When all of the particles break their forces of attraction, the liquid turns into a gas. We call this **boiling**. The temperature of the boiling point can be affected by a number of conditions, such as the presence of other substances in the liquid or the altitude at which the water is being heated. Boiling points are very precise for pure liquids and are often used as a means of identifying substances. For example, in its pure form, water will boil at 212°F (100°C) at one atmosphere of pressure.

When heating a pan of water on the top of a mountain, the water boils at a lower temperature. At high altitudes, the air is thin because there are fewer air particles present and the air pressure is lower than at sea level. When the water is heated, there are fewer particles in the air to prevent the heated water particles from escaping.

▲ The boiling point of water changes with varying altitude. At high altitude you can make tea very quickly, but it won't be as tasty because water at a lower temperature is less efficient for brewing tea!

GASES TO LIQUIDS

When gases are cooled, the molecules lose some of their energy, they move more slowly, and the gas "condenses." As the particles lose energy, they move closer together and the forces of attraction begin to restrict their movement so that they become liquid. **Condensation** can be observed in cold weather; if we breathe onto a pane of cold glass, our warm breath condenses as the water vapor cools. Gases also form liquids when they are compressed.

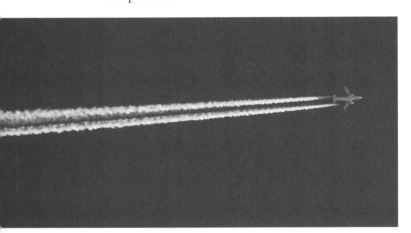

▲ The vapor trail following an airplane is formed by water droplets and ice crystals that condense on the cold exterior of the aircraft and are left behind and cooled by the air.

CHANGING BETWEEN LIQUIDS AND SOLIDS

LIQUIDS TO SOLIDS

Freezing occurs when a liquid changes into a solid. If liquid particles are cooled, they begin to form a regular structure. As they lose energy, the particles are less able to move apart.

SOLIDS TO LIQUIDS

When solids gain heat energy, the particles vibrate vigorously and can break the forces holding them together. The particles begin to behave like a liquid and **melting** occurs. The "melting point" can tell us a lot about the identity of a pure substance.

▲ Solid iodine sublimes at room temperature (see below).

CHANGING BETWEEN SOLIDS AND GASES

Solids can also be converted into gases, and gases to solids, without a liquid stage in between. This process is called **sublimation**, and it is quite rare. "Stage smoke" uses the principle of sublimation. It is made from frozen carbon dioxide gas, called "dry ice," that sublimes to produce a smoky effect. While these physical changes are taking place, the amount of the substance does not change—it simply changes from one physical state to another.

DID YOU KNOW?

▶ When water freezes, its volume increases. The same number of particles occupy more space, which is why ice is less dense than water. This phenomenon can cause problems at home in the winter. During cold weather, water in pipes can freeze and expand—and if the pipes burst, the water will flood a home. Using insulation around the pipes helps keep them warm enough to prevent freezing.

▶ The water under the Arctic ice is close to freezing but some fish have adapted to survive there. They produce a molecule in their blood that is similar to the antifreeze that people put in car engines. This helps the fish survive in conditions that would freeze other creatures.

▶ Terrorists attempted to attack the London Underground system on July 21, 2005, but the explosive failed to detonate. Experts believe this was because the explosive was a substance that sublimes at room temperature.

A CLOSER LOOK AT PHYSICAL CHANGES

The three states of matter (solids, liquids, and gases) can be altered by any one physical change. These are summarized by the triangle below.

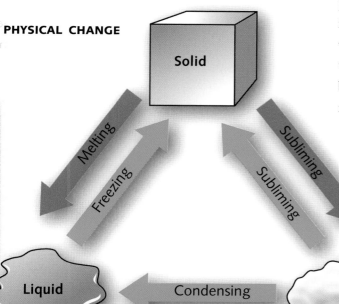

PHYSICAL CHANGE

DIFFERENT TYPES OF SOLIDS

Although the particles in a solid are tightly bound, variations in these patterns can explain why some solids float while others sink. Compare the behavior of a piece of metal and a piece of plastic when they are placed in a large tank of water. It would not be unreasonable to assume that the

piece of metal would sink, while the piece of plastic would float. This is because metal and plastic have different densities.

In metals, the particles are held tightly together with few spaces between them. This tight structure means that a greater number of metal particles are packed into one area and the material is described as dense. Dense solids will sink in water because their density is greater than that of the water. The particles in plastics are also tightly bound, making the material a solid. However, the rows of particles have spaces between them. This means that plastic has a lower density than metal. Plastic will float in water if its density is lower than that of the water.

HEATING SOLIDS

Most solids **expand** just before they reach their melting point and turn into a liquid. This is because the particles start to move apart as the forces of attraction become weaker. Some metal bridges have small gaps between their metal parts. On hot days, the increased heat energy will cause the metal particles to vibrate more than usual and the metal will slightly expand. Small gaps allow for this natural movement and help maintain the shape and structure of the bridge. When the weather cools, the metal **contracts**.

Heating gases

Like solids, gases also expand and contract. The particles in hot gases have more energy than those in cold gases, and as the hot gas particles move vigorously, they occupy a greater volume. This can have useful applications. For example, a blast of hot air that is less dense than the surrounding air can lift a hot air balloon.

Gas pressure

Gas particles move randomly, and they collide with each other and the sides of the container in which they are stored. Each time a particle rebounds off the container it exerts a small amount of pressure—caused by a transfer of energy from the particle to the wall of the container. Gas pressure can be increased in the following ways:

▶ Increasing the temperature gives the gas particles more energy, which also increases both the frequency and the force of each collision. Gas pressure will increase at higher temperatures.

▶ Decreasing the volume or increasing the pressure compresses a gas because the same number of gas particles occupy a smaller space. This means that the frequency of collisions—and therefore the pressure—will be increased. If a gas is compressed quickly, its temperature will rise, which adds to the increasing pressure.

▲ The gas in a hot air balloon cools as the balloon moves higher. If the gas volume decreases, the balloon will sink again.

Test yourself

▶ Why do balloons burst if you keep blowing air into them?
▶ If a gas is transferred from a small container to a larger one, what happens to the pressure?

34

Mixtures and compounds

7

When elements are combined, they form either a mixture or a compound. Compounds are formed by chemical reactions that usually require heat energy. For example, if the elements iron and sulfur are combined without heating, we have a mixture of iron and sulfur. However, if these two elements are combined and heated, we form a compound called iron sulfide.

MIXTURES OR COMPOUNDS

A mixture is two or more elements combined, which can be separated again by physical means. A mixture can be compared to a sample of red and blue marbles. We can clearly see the properties of the marbles and can easily separate them. In contrast, a compound is two or more elements chemically combined. A compound is formed when the atoms of various elements donate, receive, or share electrons to form molecules. This is called chemical bonding.

A mixture displays the same properties as the individual elements from which it is made. In contrast, a compound has new, unique properties. For example, an iron and sulfur mixture looks like a combination of yellow and gray powders but can easily be separated using a magnet. In contrast, iron sulfide has a completely new appearance (a black solid) and is not magnetic. Iron sulfide can only be separated using another chemical process that breaks the newly formed bonds. This is because the iron atoms have donated some of the electrons from their outer shells to the sulfur atoms to form a chemical compound.

▼ A mixture of iron and sulfur can be separated using a magnet because the iron is attracted to the magnetic force.

TYPES OF MIXTURES

SOLID/SOLID MIXTURES

Mixtures of this kind are made from different solids. Sand and soil are two examples. Soil is made up of different types of particles and sand contains small sand particles as well as parts of shells and larger pebbles. These examples are mixtures because heat was not involved in their formation and the particles can easily be separated.

SOLID/LIQUID MIXTURES

When it rains heavily, soil can mix with the rainwater to form a muddy liquid. This is also a mixture because no heat is involved and no chemical reactions have taken place. If you look closely at a muddy puddle, you may see small particles of soil floating in it. This is called a suspension. The soil particles can be easily separated from the water.

SOLID/GAS MIXTURES

Solids and gases can also form mixtures. Sometimes, the exterior walls of houses or buildings are cleaned using a sandblasting technique. The dust that comes off the walls is very fine and mixes with the surrounding air. This dust will eventually settle and become separated from the air. A similar observation is made when a car drives down a dusty road. Dust from the road is scattered into the air creating a mixture of air and dust particles. Nature also provides us with examples of solid/gas mixtures. During volcanic eruptions, for example, the exploding flow of ash and rock is a highly dangerous, hot mixture of solid and gas material.

TEST YOURSELF

▶ What combination of physical states have made the following mixtures?

(1) Shaving foam

(2) A cup of coffee with cream, but no sugar

(3) A cup of coffee with cream and sugar

(4) A coin

LIQUID/LIQUID AND LIQUID/GAS MIXTURES

What happens when we make orange juice by mixing concentrated orange juice with water? We make a mixture from these two liquids. This process does not involve heat, no chemical bonds have formed, and the two liquids can be separated from each other. Carbonated drinks, such as soda pop, are examples of liquid/gas mixtures. Carbonation occurs when manufacturers inject carbon dioxide gas into the liquid. The liquid and gas can be separated again by leaving the bottle uncovered. It may take a few days, but eventually the drink becomes "flat."

TYPES OF COMPOUNDS

Compounds, like mixtures, are composed of at least two different elements. However, unlike mixtures, compounds are formed when energy causes a chemical reaction. This energy is usually heat, but chemists also use electricity, light, or even the energy stored in other chemicals. A chemical reaction forces the elements to bond by rearranging their electrons to create more stable products. This makes them difficult to separate.

◀ A volcanic eruption can throw millions of tons of ash into the air.

Compounds display completely new properties. For example, water is a colorless liquid made from the elements hydrogen and oxygen, both colorless and odorless gases. Compounds differ from mixtures because they:

▶ need a chemical reaction to form.
▶ can only be separated by using another chemical reaction.
▶ do not necessarily have the same properties as their constituent elements.
▶ contain the constituent elements in definite proportions. For instance, water always contains twice as much hydrogen as oxygen (H_2O).

NONMETAL BONDING

Elements bond in a number of different ways. Nonmetals bond by sharing electrons. Atoms will try to maximize the number of electrons in their outer shells when they bond; the best way for nonmetals to do this is by sharing electrons. For example, water (H_2O) has two hydrogen atoms and one oxygen atom. Oxygen has six electrons in its outer (second) shell and to achieve the full complement of eight, it shares two electrons with a hydrogen atom. This is called covalent bonding.

METAL AND NONMETAL BONDING

A metal and a nonmetal will bond by donating and receiving electrons. Salt is an example of a metal and nonmetal compound of sodium and chlorine.

Sodium has one electron in its outer shell and chlorine has seven. However, both of these atoms can gain the full complement of electrons on their outer shell if sodium gives its "spare" electron to chlorine. This is called ionic bonding.

NAMING COMPOUNDS

There is no systematic way of naming compounds made from two nonmetallic elements—many of the names simply have to be learned. Chemists around the world use formulas for the compounds they are working with. This creates a common language for all scientists. The table, below, shows some familiar compounds with their names and formulas.

Hydrogen chloride	HCl
Water	H_2O
Carbon monoxide	CO
Carbon dioxide	CO_2
Ammonia	NH_3
Ammonium chloride	NH_4Cl
Hydrochloric acid	HCl
Sulfuric acid	H_2SO_4
Nitric acid	HNO_3
Methane	CH_4

COMPOUNDS FROM METALS AND NONMETALS

When atoms gain or lose electrons, they become charged. Certain atoms will always form the same charge. For example, aluminum always loses three electrons when it forms a compound; so, we say that it has a 3+ charge. Compounds that are formed from these charged atoms are called **ions**. Some common ions are shown in the table, below.

Charge 3+	Charge 2+	Charge 1+	Charge 1-	Charge 2-
(aluminum) Al^{3+}	(magnesium) Mg^{2+}	(hydrogen) H^+	(hydroxide) OH^-	(oxide) O^{2-}
(chromium) Cr^{3+}	(calcium) Ca^{2+}	(sodium) Na^+	(chloride) Cl^-	(sulfide) S^{2-}
(iron) Fe^{3+}	(copper) Cu^{2+}	(lithium) Li^+	(iodide) I^-	(sulfate) SO_4^{2-}

When ions are combined, we use a technique called "swap and drop" to determine the formula of the new compound. Swap and drop is conducted in the following way:

(1) Write the symbol for each of the ions involved and their charges beneath them. For example, a compound of hydrogen and sulfide would be written as:

$$\textbf{H} \quad \textbf{S}$$
$$\textbf{1} \quad \textbf{2}$$

(2) Swap and drop these numbers as shown below.

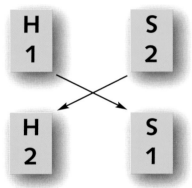

(3) The numbers in the second row tell us that the formula has two hydrogen (H) atoms and one sulfide (S) atom. This is written as H_2S. The name for this compound is hydrogen sulfide—a combination of the two names.

TEST YOURSELF

▶ Using the swap and drop technique, determine the formula and name for each of the following combinations of ions.

1. Sodium and hydroxide

2. Magnesium and chloride

3. Calcium and oxide

UNEXPECTED DISCOVERIES

Sometimes during their laboratory work, scientists make new discoveries about useful compounds. The following historical examples introduced some of the compounds that we commonly use today.

DYES

In 1856, a chemist's assistant named William Perkin was asked to prepare a synthetic anti-malarial drug, called quinine. At the time, Perkin was only 18 years old and had little laboratory experience. He was working with a product made from coal tar, but instead of producing quinine, he created a mysterious black substance. Perkin's curiosity led him to further explore the substance. He dissolved it in alcohol and found that it produced a stunning purple-colored solution. Perkin then discovered that the purple solution could dye fabrics, such as silk and cotton, and it did not wash out or fade in the sun. Perkin had discovered a mauve dye.

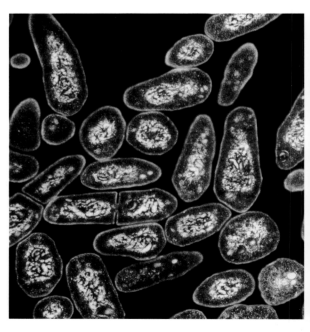

▲ Perkin's mauve dye is now used in microscopy work to color bacteria, such as cholera or tuberculosis (above).

Other dyes were also discovered by accident.
In 1928, a blue dye was isolated at a chemical
plant in Scotland. A plant worker named
Dandridge noticed during the industrial process
that blue crystals were forming on the inside of a
sealed container. The crystals were produced
when iron in the container reacted with
industrial chemicals to create a by-product called
phthalocyanine. At the time, phthalocyanine
was not fully appreciated, but 20 years later, it
was found that when copper combined with
phthalocyanine, it created a rich blue color. This
led to the discovery of a blue dye that is now
used in paints and printing inks.

NYLON

In 1930, a team of American chemists, led by
Dr. Wallace Carothers at the DuPont company,
were trying to unravel natural fibers of rubber
and silk to discover the composition of these
useful materials. The researchers hoped they
could reproduce the properties for other
synthetic materials, such as polyester.

One afternoon when Carothers was out of the
laboratory, his team of young chemists had some
fun seeing how far they could pull a fiber from a
polyester solution. They were surprised to
produce a fiber as long as the corridor outside
their lab, and they quickly realized that they
were on the verge of an important discovery.

Polyester has a very low melting point, making
it difficult to weave into fabrics. The scientists
decided to repeat the experiment on another
group of man-made materials called
polyamides. This was how nylon was discovered.
Nylon is a very popular textile; when nylon
stockings went on sale in New York in 1940, over
four million pairs were sold in a few hours!

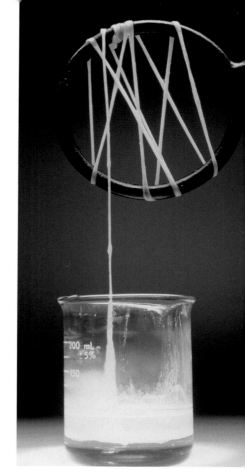

▶ Nylon is a synthetic fiber
discovered in the 1930s.
It is now used to make
fabrics, rope, and some
medical products.

SILK

Silk is a natural fiber
harvested from the
cocoons of silkworm
caterpillars. During the
1870s, French scientist
Louis Pasteur was asked
to investigate a disease
that killed silkworms,
threatening to ruin the
French silk industry. One
day, Pasteur's young
assistant, Chardonnet, accidentally spilled a
substance in the laboratory and left the lab
without wiping up the spill. On his return, he
discovered that the spilled substance had turned
fibrous and resembled the structure of silk.
Chardonnet experimented further and discovered
the compound rayon.

INVESTIGATE

▶ Research the discovery of penicillin by Alexander
Fleming with the following questions in mind.

1. How much of the discovery was due to luck?

2. How has Fleming's discovery been used today?
What have its disadvantages been?

3. What aspects of Fleming's discovery have
been developed further?

TIME TRAVEL: INTO THE FUTURE

Compounds are all around us and can be found as solids, liquids, or gases. There are many uses for everyday compounds. However, despite the wealth of materials already at our disposal, chemists are always researching new materials that could be useful in our daily lives.

SYNTHETIC DIAMONDS

Diamond is a precious mineral that is difficult to find, buried hundreds of miles below the earth's surface. It is made from the element carbon that becomes heated under great pressure, during the earth's natural geological cycle.

In recent years, chemists have successfully replicated these natural conditions in a laboratory to make synthetic diamonds. The first synthetic diamond was made in 1954 when scientists subjected graphite to

extreme temperature and pressure conditions. However, the experiment required so much electricity that it was cheaper to buy an actual diamond! Today, synthetic diamonds can be made more cheaply. They can be used for jewelry but are also used extensively in industry to make durable cutting tools. Synthetic diamonds are also a useful material for the microelectronics industry—they are extremely hard-wearing and can be shaped into minute pieces, without breaking.

SELF-CLEANING WINDOWS

A compound called titanium dioxide (TiO_2) has been developed by a team of researchers at the University of Texas to create self-cleaning windows. When sunlight hits the titanium dioxide coating, the electrons gain energy and move away from the titanium dioxide compound. In turn, this creates **free radicals** that react with dirt on the window, cleaning the glass, and preventing it from fogging. Self-cleaning glass is not currently on the market, but the technology has enormous potential.

NONSTICKING PLASTICS

Scientists at the Dow Chemical Company have developed a plastic nonstick coating that cannot be written on, and it repels water and other liquids. The plastic is mostly composed of carbon, which is combined with atoms of the element fluorine. The fluorine atoms are positioned on the outside of the plastic; it is these atoms that prevent substances from sticking. Dow is researching possible uses of their new plastic in hospitals, on kitchen and bathroom surfaces, and as a deicing material for aircraft wings. The plastic could also be used in artificial heart valves to prevent the formation of blood clots. At present, the plastic is damaged at high temperatures, so it cannot be used in some cooking utensils.

▲ A nonstick plastic coating on this wall could prevent it from becoming covered with graffiti.

DID YOU KNOW?

▶ A company in Chicago charges $4,000 to $22,000 to turn the ashes of cremated human remains, which are primarily carbon, into synthetic diamonds. The process has taken three years to perfect. It involves the purification of cremation ashes at temperatures of 5,432°F (3,000°C), followed by more heat and pressure. This process forms a synthetic diamond in about 16 weeks. The longer the process continues, the higher the quality of the diamond produced.

Separating mixtures

8

Mixtures are created when two or more elements are combined without a chemical reaction. Unlike compounds, mixtures can be separated using a variety of simple techniques. Two common separation techniques used by chemists today are evaporation and **distillation**.

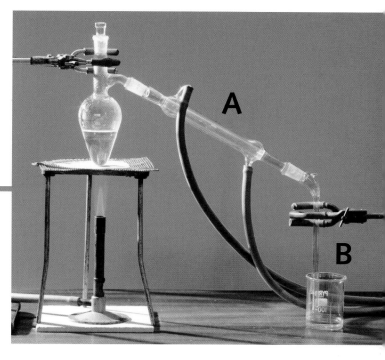

▲ Distillation equipment can be used to separate mixtures that have different boiling points.

EVAPORATION

When a solid is dissolved in water, its elements can be separated through evaporation, while retaining the solid component. For example, seawater has salt dissolved in it. If the seawater is heated so that the water boils away, a white residue is left behind that can be tested and determined to be salt. If you swim in the sea and allow your skin to dry in the sun, you may find white deposits on your skin. These are salt deposits from the seawater.

DISTILLATION

To retain both parts of a solution, chemists use the distillation process. Distillation can also separate two liquids. Liquid mixtures can be separated using the distillation equipment shown above. If the mixture is heated, the components with the lowest boiling points will boil first, and leave the liquid mixture as a gas. The vapors will travel to the condenser at the top (A) and condense into a liquid as they are cooled. The condensed liquid will then travel to the collecting beaker (B). Distillation equipment has the following features that cause liquids to become separated:

▶ The condenser is surrounded by a cold water jacket, connected to a tap. Cold water is constantly flowing from the bottom of the condenser toward the top. This means that the condenser is never warmed by the rising hot vapors and will always remain cold.

▶ The heated end of the equipment is usually placed higher than the collecting end so that gravity can help the condensed vapors flow into the collecting vessel.

▶ Sometimes, a thermometer is used to indicate the boiling point of the component that has evaporated. This is useful for identification purposes. For example, in the simple distillation of soda pop, the component that boils off first—the distillate—has a boiling point of 212°F (100°C) and is identified as water.

Note: You must have an adult's permission for the following experiment.

▶ Make a salt solution by dissolving some common table salt in warm water. Make sure you dissolve enough salt so that the solution tastes salty. Put the salt water solution in a dish that can sit over a saucepan of water, without touching the water. Gently simmer the water so that the salt solution begins to evaporate. When you see a white residue on the sides of the dish, remove it from the heat. Leave the dish in a sunny window for up to one week.

▶ What can you see after one week? If the dish is used for eating, taste the white residue. What do you notice?

INDUSTRIAL SEPARATION PROCESSES

Many of the products we use in everyday life come from crude oil—the remains of ancient plants and animals found deep beneath the earth's surface. Crude oil forms when these remains become buried, crushed, and heated throughout millions of years. The term "crude" denotes a mixture; crude oil is a mixture of many useful components. However, it is not possible to separate these through simple distillation. Instead, crude oil is separated by a process called **fractional distillation**.

SEPARATING CRUDE OIL

The equipment needed for fractional distillation is similar to that of simple distillation—both involve heating components to their boiling points and collecting the vapors for condensing. We call each component that is extracted a "fraction."

During fractional distillation, crude oil is passed through the bottom of a column and heated slowly. The fractions of the oil with the lowest boiling points evaporate first and travel to the top of the column where it is cooler. Here, they condense and are collected on small trays, to prevent them from falling to the bottom of the column again. The condensing process slightly heats this top area of the column.

Meanwhile, the remainder of the crude oil is heated further so that the fraction with the second lowest boiling point evaporates. This vapor travels to the point near the top of the column where it is coolest—just below the first fraction—and condensation and collection occur again. This process continues until eight separate fractions of oil have been collected.

REFINING CRUDE OIL

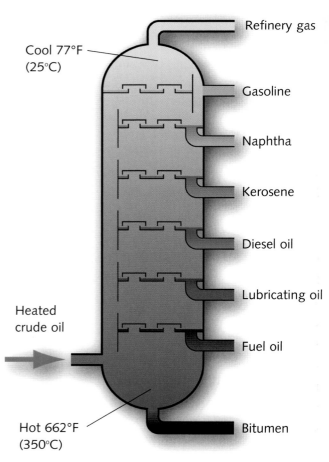

Refinery gas

Cool 77°F (25°C)

Gasoline

Naphtha

Kerosene

Diesel oil

Lubricating oil

Heated crude oil

Fuel oil

Hot 662°F (350°C)

Bitumen

At the end of distillation, the fractionating column is cooler at the top than at the bottom. This is because the fractions condensing at the bottom have the highest boiling points, and as they condense, they release some of their heat. The process of separating oil by distillation is called refining.

The fractions of crude oil are summarized below:

Fraction	Boiling temperature °F (°C)	Amount produced (%)	Use
Refinery gas	<77 (< 25)	2.1	Fuels
Gasoline	104–167 (40–75)	31	Car fuel
Naphtha	167–302 (75–150)	4	Chemicals
Kerosene	302–464 (150–240)	10.6	Aviation fuel
Diesel oil	428–482 (220–250)	30.2	Diesel engine vehicles
Lubricating oil	482–662 (250–350)	1.7	Machine oil
Fuel oil	482–662 (250–350)	18	Industrial heating
Bitumen	> 662 (> 350)	2.4	Road tar

a process called "cracking." Much of the work at an oil refinery involves converting the crude oil into as many useful products as possible.

CRUDE OIL FACTS

The demand for crude oil means that its distillation must be a continuous process. The differing proportions of fractions produced can affect the price of the products made from them. For example, in the U.S., there were approximately 21 million barrels of crude oil extracted in 2004; this was down 9 percent from the previous year. In fact, statistics show that supplies of extractable crude oil reserves are falling each year.

The number of fractions produced depends on the natural forces that formed the oil in the first place and where the oil is extracted. For example, North Sea oil produces about 6 percent gasoline and 19 percent diesel oil. Some South American crude oil contains only 10 percent diesel oil and the remainder are the fractions that boil at higher temperatures. Fuel companies have developed ways to make more useful fractions from some of the other oil products; gasoline can be made from some of these higher boiling fractions by

DID YOU KNOW?

▶ Sometimes, materials decompose when they are subjected to high temperatures, making it difficult to separate them from each other. These mixtures can be distilled using a technique called vacuum distillation. A pump is used to reduce some of the air pressure in the equipment so that the liquids boil at lower temperatures, making the mixtures less likely to decompose.

▶ Scientists have discovered ways to convert coal into oil. Oil reserves are quickly running out. Converting large coal reserves into oil would be an alternate source of fuel, while other alternative energy sources are being researched. Coal is converted using a technique called the "Fischer-Tropsch" process. In South Africa, the Sasol company utilizes this process to produce most of the country's diesel fuel.

CHROMATOGRAPHY

Some mixtures, such as ink, can be separated by a technique called **chromatography**. Chromatography can take a number of different forms but all have certain features in common. All types of chromatography need a substance to act as a solvent to dissolve the mixture that is being separated. The technique also requires a surface through which the dissolved mixture can travel. In the case of simple chromatography, this surface is paper.

SEPARATING INK

The ink that people use in their fountain pens is actually a mixture of different colored pigments that give the ink its final color. If you use a fountain pen, you may already realize the importance of not getting the page wet—the ink runs and the writing becomes smudged. Fountain pen ink dissolves in water, which is the solvent that can be used in this type of chromatography.

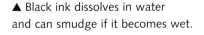

▲ Black ink dissolves in water and can smudge if it becomes wet.

Chromatography works according to the principle that the components of a mixture dissolve in a solvent to varying degrees—each component is retained to a greater or lesser degree by the surface through which it is traveling. Some components are highly soluble and will remain in the solution much longer than less soluble components. As the dissolved mixture travels through the surface material, the components are deposited at different levels and the mixture becomes separated. If paper is used, a streak appears on its surface in varying

colors. The results of chromatography are called chromatograms. The following experiment can be used to separate the colors of ink:

(1) Draw a line in pencil just above the bottom of a strip of filter paper. This marks the position of the ink so we can measure with a ruler how far the different components have traveled. The line must be drawn with a pencil because other types of ink may interfere with the process.

(2) Drop a small spot of ink onto the pencil line.

(3) Place the filter paper into a beaker of water so that the water line falls just below the pencil line. The water molecules are attracted to the absorbent filter paper and are pulled up the paper. When the first molecules leave the water, the next molecules follow because they are also attracted to the paper; this is called capillary action. The chromatography is completed when the water stops moving, or has reached the top of the paper.

CHROMATOGRAM

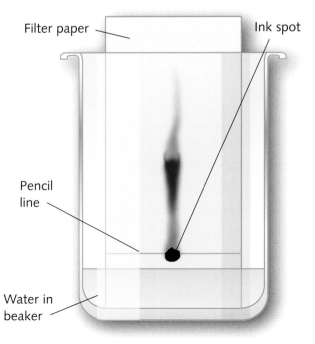

Filter paper

Ink spot

Pencil line

Water in beaker

OTHER TYPES OF CHROMATOGRAPHY

Chemists often use chromatography to identify the components present in mixtures and to see how pure they are. Sometimes, forensic scientists use the same principles to match substances from crime scenes, such as paint pigments or drugs. In recent years, chromatography has advanced with the aid of computer technology. Computers enable scientists to separate complex mixtures and to identify the components with greater accuracy.

INVESTIGATE

▶ Using absorbent paper, such as filter paper, investigate the colors that different colored candy, such as Skittles or M&Ms, contain in their coatings.

(1) Leave different colored candies in water so that some of the color is removed.

(2) Draw a line in pencil across the bottom of the filter paper.

(3) Place some of the colored pigment onto the line using a fine instrument, such as a thin straw.

(4) Place the filter paper into a clear container of water so that the pencil line sits above the water line.

(5) Observe the water movement until it stops or reaches the top.

(6) Remove the paper and allow it to dry.

(7) Examine the chromatograms and identify the different colors in the candy coating.

◀ Forensic scientists use chromatography to identify the different substances present at the scene of a crime.

TEST YOURSELF

▶ A team of forensic scientists wish to match the paint pigment found at the scene of a crime with the pigment from the cars of three suspects. The chromatograms are shown below.

Which suspect would the forensic scientists tell the police about and which could they eliminate? Explain your answers.

(1) Sample from the crime scene   (2) Suspect A   (3) Suspect B   (4) Suspect C

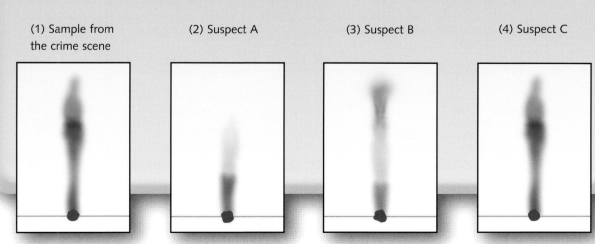

Glossary

ALCHEMY – The medieval study of chemistry.

ALPHA PARTICLES – Particles that contain two neutrons and two protons.

ATOM – The simplest form of a particle.

ATOMIC NUMBER – The number of protons in an atom of an element.

BOILING – Changing from a liquid to a gas.

BONDING – Joining together of two or more atoms through a chemical reaction.

BROWNIAN MOTION – The random movement of particles in air or a liquid, first observed through a microscope by Robert Brown in 1827.

CHROMATOGRAPHY – A method of separating mixtures using a solvent.

COMPOUND – A substance made from at least two chemically bonded elements.

CONDENSATION – Changing from a gas to a liquid. Condensation occurs when gases are cooled.

CONTRACT – When a material becomes smaller.

DENSITY – A measure of mass per unit volume.

DISTILLATION – Separating a substance through boiling and cooling.

ELECTRON – The negative part of an atom. Electrons travel in shells.

ELECTRON CONFIGURATION – The arrangement of electrons in an atom.

EVAPORATION – Changing from a liquid to a gas at the surface of the liquid.

EXPAND – When a material becomes larger.

FRACTIONAL DISTILLATION – Separating several substances through boiling.

FREE RADICALS – Particles containing electrons that are unpaired.

ANSWERS

Page 12: Investigate
(1) Magnesium – atomic number 12, mass number 24 (12 protons, 12 electrons, 12 neutrons)

(2) Bromine – atomic number 35, mass number 80 (35 protons, 35 electrons, 45 neutrons)

(3) Neon – atomic number 10, mass number 20 (10 protons, 10 electrons, 10 neutrons)

Page 15: Test yourself
Aluminum has 13 protons (and therefore 13 electrons). The first shell has 2 electrons (the maximum) with 11 remaining. The second shell has 8 electrons (the maximum) and 3 remaining. The third shell contains the remaining 3 electrons and is not completely full. The electron configuration for aluminum is 2,8,3.

Page 15: Investigate
(1) Neon – atomic number 10, electron configuration 2,8.
(2) Magnesium – atomic number 12, electron configuration 2,8,2.
(3) Calcium – atomic number 20, electron configuration 2,8,10.
(4) Chlorine – atomic number 17, electron configuration 2,8,7.
(5) Sodium – atomic number 11, electron configuration 2,8,1.

Page 17: Test yourself
(1) Jelly – wobbles and not very strong; can be poured when heated.
(2) Paste – can be spread on paper, but when set, becomes hard like a solid.
(3) Glue stick – in the tube it is solid, but when rubbed across paper, a sticky residue is left behind.

Page 23: Investigate
(1) Na – Sodium   (5) Scandium – Sc
(2) Mg – Magnesium   (6) Sulfur – S
(3) Zn – Zinc   (7) Antimony – Sb
(4) I – Iodine   (8) Lead – Pb

Page 25: Investigate
You should find that your predictions are generally correct, but that the properties are either more exaggerated for groups on the left or less exaggerated for groups on the right (as you go down the group).

Page 27: Investigate
Argon (Ar) and potassium (K); cobalt (Co) and nickel (Ni); thorium (Th) and protactinium (Pa).

Page 33: Investigate
You should find that the mass is approximately the

FREEZING – Changing from a liquid to a solid.

FUSION – The bonding of nuclei.

GROUP – A vertical collection of elements in the periodic table.

INTERMOLECULAR – Between molecules.

IONS – Particles with either a positive or negative charge.

MASS NUMBER – The number of protons and neutrons in an atom.

MELTING – Changing from a solid to a liquid.

MOLECULE – At least two chemically bonded atoms.

NEUTRINO – An elementary particle.

NEUTRON – The part of a nucleus with a neutral charge.

NUCLEUS – The center of an atom containing neutrons and protons.

PERIOD – A horizontal collection of elements in the periodic table.

PERIODIC TABLE – A table showing all of the chemical elements.

PROTON – The positive part of an atom, found in the nucleus.

RADIOACTIVE – The decomposition of atoms through natural processes.

SUBLIMATION – Changing directly from a solid to a gas, or the other way around.

VOLATILE – Easily evaporated.

Useful Web sites:
www.chem4kids.com
www.sciencenewsforkids.org
www.newscientist.com
www.howstuffworks.com
www.chemtutor.com/index.html

---

same, but the volume is much greater in ice than in water.

Page 33: Test yourself
(1) Condensation
(2) Evaporation

Page 34: Test yourself
As you blow into the balloon, the number of air particles inside multiplies and the pressure increases. Eventually, the pressure is too great to contain the air particles and the balloon bursts.

The same number of particles occupy a larger space, so the number of collisions with the walls of the container are reduced. This reduces the pressure.

Page 36: Test yourself
(1) Shaving foam – gas/liquid.
(2) Coffee with cream, no sugar – liquid/liquid.

(3) Coffee with cream and sugar – liquid/liquid and liquid/solid.
(4) Coin – solid/solid.

Page 38: Test yourself
(1) Sodium and hydroxide (NaOH – sodium hydroxide).
(2) Magnesium and chloride ($MgCl_2$ – magnesium chloride).
(3) Calcium and oxide (CaO – calcium oxide).

Page 39: Investigate
(1) Fleming left a petri dish on a window sill and mold grew in his absence.
(2) Antibiotics have saved lives all over the world, but resistance is becoming common because many antibiotics have been overused. For example, bacteria become resistant to antibiotics that are given to animals and pass to humans through the food chain.

(3) Chemists use the structure of the original penicillin and synthesize similar compounds. These drugs are just as effective, and bacteria are not resistant to them.

Page 42: Investigate
You will probably observe white crystals that taste salty.

Page 45: Investigate
Darker colors, such as brown, will contain more colors than the lighter colors, such as yellow.

Page 45: Test yourself
Suspect C should be arrested because the chromatogram is exactly the same as the sample from the crime scene. Suspect A is eliminated because there is a light blue color present, and no red/pink. Suspect B is eliminated because there is a light blue color present.

Index

Page references in *italics* represent pictures.

DATE DUE

Demco, Inc. 38-293